A Word for All Seasons

The opinions expressed in this manuscript are solely the opinions of the authors and do nor represent the opinions or thoughts of the publisher. The authors have represented and warranted full ownership and/or legal right to publish all the materials in this book.

A Word For All Seasons
Anthology Number Five
All Rights Reserved
Copyright @2014 Benicia First Tuesday Poets
Published by Benicia Literary Arts
Benicia, California
www.benicialiteraryarts.org

ISBN 978-0-9703737-1-7
Library of Congress Control Number 2013921829

Produced by Benicia Literary Arts, which encourages reading and writing in the community by producing events, creating a community of writers and readers, encouraging their development, and publishing works of high quality in all genres. The organization's website is www.benicialiteraryarts.org.

Cover Art and Design by Thomas Eric Stanton
Design and layout by Thomas Eric Stanton
Edited by Lois Requist and Sherry Sheehan

Special thanks to former poets laureate Joel Fallon, Ronna Leon, and Robert Shelby for their invaluable help in making this anthology possible.

This book may not be reproduced, transmitted, or stored in whole or in part by any means, including graphic, electronic, or mechanical, without the express written consent of the publisher except in the case of brief quotations embodied in critical articles and reviews.

Please note: Poems have been printed exactly as submitted without further editing.

Contents

- 1. *Ronna Leon*
- 5. *Alice Salerno*
- 9. *Thomas Eric Stanton*
- 13. *Johanna Ely*
- 17. *Joel Fallon*
- 21. *Don Peery*
- 25. *Carol Smiles*
- 29. *John Goory*
- 33. *Genea S. Brice*
- 37. *Sherry Sheehan*
- 41. *Jady Montgomery*
- 45. *Deborah L. Fruchey*
- 49. *Linda R. Toby*
- 53. *Bonnie Weidel*
- 57. *Robert Shelby*
- 61. *Frances Jackson*
- 65. *Bobbie C. Richardson*
- 69. *Michael R. Merris*
- 73. *Peter Bray*
- 77. *Juanita J. Martin*
- 81. *Pandora Bethea*
- 85. *Colin Amato*
- 89. *Carole Dwinell*
- 93. *Jonathan Pasco, Sr.*
- 97. *Carol Hogan*
- 101. *Lois Requist*
- 105. *Brett Hudson*
- 109. *Joanette Sorkin*
- 113. *Deborah B. Silverman*

Foreword

The Benicia First Tuesday Poets have been meeting for many years. Along with the work and influence of the poet laureate program and, now, Benicia Literary Arts, poetry has become a visible force in Benicia, partnering with arts and commercial interests to enliven the already active arts scene in the community.

This fifth anthology by Benicia poets, like previous volumes, represents a wide variety of skills, development, and perspective on the part of the participants. In addition, the number of out-of-town poets published here illustrates the reach and influence of our vibrant poetry community.

A Word For All Seasons was my attempt to encourage poets to express their world in whatever variety serves them, in all its complexities, diversities, challenges, and beauty. In the Biblical words from Ecclesiastes, "to everything there is a season, and a time for every purpose..."

Robert Shelby's classical background is expressed here, as is
Bobby Richardson's strident cries for justice for people of color.
So many visions and each so unique! I think of Peter Bray, John Goory,
Frances Jackson, Jady Montgomery, Sherry Sheehan, and
Thomas Eric Stanton.
Some of these views make us uncomfortable.
They should!

Poetry reaches into the corners of our conscious and unconscious mind, tickling something almost inexpressible, expanding our view of what is possible in a war worn, weary and often cynical world.

Here's to poetry and to the poets represented in this volume! May our world be better, in even a small way, because of it!

Lois Requist, Benicia Poet Laureate, 2012-2014

Ronna Leon

Since 1983 Ronna Leon and husband Joe have lived in Benicia, where they raised three of their four sons. They are the proud grandparents of five grandsons and one new granddaughter whom they hope to spoil endlessly. Ronna served as Benicia's third poet laureate from 2010 to 2012. She currently directs Arts Benicia's printmaking studio.

Sibling Ties

Over fifty years ago we lived together, my sisters and I,
in a house that got remodeled into something grander long ago
by another family, in a town that changed with the times.
All our shared memories seem quaint, are quaint and smell
of clothes hung on the line and chalk instead of computers.
Our bikes had baskets and bells that honked
or trilled with a push of the thumb.
No fast food or chain stores but Sears and Woolworth.
We carried our lunches in brown
paper sacks and had glass-lined thermoses that shattered when dropped.
Each Friday, if we'd been good, we got a dime for eskimo pie ice cream bars.
We had daily chores. We had company manners.
We read books and memorized poems and listened
to radio soap operas and mystery stories.
"The Shadow Knows," we'd warn each other.
We played cards and board games and did wooden jigsaw puzzles.
Almost nothing of the world we had in common from childhood remains.
Our parents are long dead.
Our grown-up lives drew us to distant lands and different experiences.
We stayed in touch but weren't intimate.
But now, as our old age arrives we've grown closer,
protective, curious, like the children we once were.
In each other we treasure the past only we had
and touch together our nearing future.

Ronna Leon

Report

The moods of love control my life like weather:
Chill damp followed by clearing.
Unsettled fronts give way to warming trends.
Like to the weather, I submit,
Bundle up the best I can,
Carry a red umbrella,
Try to remember my hat.

Still caught by surprise
In spring storms, first snows,
Unrelenting heat waves -
Love overtakes all preparations
Strategies of sense
Soaks me through and through,
Pushes me to walk in moonlight,
Gave me you, to cling to,
In the fiery confusion of Santa Ana winds.

Dave's Wake

My teetotaling friend held the wake
   for the town's drunk.
He died of complications
   his girlfriend was too addled to interpret.

Dave had been her husband's friend.
She told them to put the alcohol
   outside on the porch.

In the gray afternoon fog and cigarette smoke
   her winter oranges glowed.

Dave's son cried reading a letter the lawyer brought.
His father had written it when the boy was three
making promises he couldn't keep
  even in more sober times.
More than one guest declared
  that the dead man told them
  their hostess had said,
"You are a slave to alcohol, Dave."
It was the common toast
the company drank to deeply
   all afternoon.

Later, my friend sat in my living room
instructing me on her own funeral -
ten minutes of hymns, no minister speaking,
the wake at her house with people who knew her.
We might say, "She was kind and funny."
That would be enough.
But "No alcohol, NONE!"

I listen, nod but think,
"Oh my dear, dear friend,
the day you die, that day your true goodness ends,
on that dismal day, forgive me,
for surely I'll take to drink and tie one on.

Ronna Leon

Alice Salerno

Alice Salerno has worked as wife, mom, graphic artist, window designer, retail advertising manager, interior design consultant, 3-state advertising director for two international retail firms, and director of her own advertising and public relations agency. Obviously, none of these occupations were related to poetry. Poetry simply runs along beside Salerno's life, like a quiet river beside a busy road.

Winter

We inhale
uneasily for the time it takes
to turn over
in the death of winter

I do not know...
I haven't asked before...
does Bear ever sleep in summer
or lie down a bit in spring?

Or does she roam
with blood and juice on her jaws
flailing her random arms
unremittingly
until it snows again?

Alice Salerno

Invasion

Spring surprised the foothills
this morning
overwhelming them with riot green.

Wild mustard swept through meadows
establishing control in orchards, encountering
only token resistance from
trees already infiltrated by pale buds.

Grey clouds threaten retaliation
from a safe distance
but sunlight sneaks around their borders
dispensing victory propaganda.

Storm Warning

The jagged cliffs of his unloving
thrust into his soul's inlets.

Soft waves of tenderness and yearning
cannot move him, cannot erode
his rocky resentments or wear away
his looming spite.

Perhaps what's needed is a great and awesome
maelstrom of loving to lash his granite powerfully
cleave deep into his molten core
and settle in a deep, new pool of caring
beside the pool of him.

Blackbirds

blackbirds light
to sift through rainbows
for sympathy seeds and metal music

sporting night-blue crowns
and stroking ebony-kettle aprons
for fruity-flavored pockets
before unzipping their harsh throats
into ebony-feathered jazz

Thomas Eric Stanton

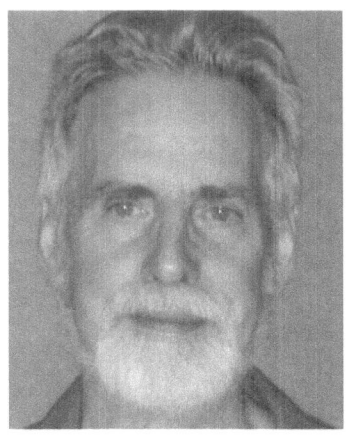

Thomas Eric Stanton graduated with an MFA in Writing and Criticism and a BA in Media Arts from The University of California at Irvine where he studied with Conceptual Artists and writers Bas Jan Ader, David Askevold and Benar Venet. He attended The Claremont Graduate University where he had the pleasure of studying with the sound artist Michael Brewster. He has read and taught in San Francisco, Los Angeles and New York. He is a visual Artist as well and has Artworks in Museum, Public and Private collections. In the late 1960s after serving with the U.S. Merchant Marine. He returned home with tape machines and discovered the wonders of Sound Art and considers himself a 'Performing Poet'.

Beige

Sitting together on old third hand couch
her glass of wine tilting precariously
She would rather not have the leatherette dent to her right
But she is kind
The couch is dirty
That's ok.

The glass tilts a bit to leeward, then rights itself.
This has been going on a long time
Her heart is huge,
his is tailor-made to adjust its size.
He knows,
he should leave.
He knows she made a mistake,
a long time ago;

he gets up very slowly
the glass tilting slightly to windward
and steadying itself at the knees.

A Sympathetic Stranger

we write poems to keep the gravity dust
off of our dearest images
we have a perfect right to continue.
The essence of fashion is hell,
change for change sake;
throwing money out the bunny wheel
while others
intactfully
move on
until the holy gap in the chords
of their woody boat
begin to stretch apart
exchanging light for dark
darkness for sweetness
purpled vessels
moving through liquid grief.

Thomas Eric Stanton

I have no words

I have
no words
that are
words
alone

If I could
find such
a word
it would be
quotative,
a
metaphor
for it's self

A reference
to the
secret
entity
that
created
it

Thomas Eric Stanton

With Stones in Her Pocket

It is widely known
that we cannot place
stones
in
our
pockets
until
we
are,

dedicated
to...

the
ultimate
life...

of
a
simple
poem,

murdered
by
insistence.

Thomas Eric Stanton

Johanna Ely

Johanna Ely has been writing poems since the fourth grade. Now that she is retired, she hopes to write more frequently and give voice to her "secret passion." She has lived in Benicia for 28 years. Graduating from U.C. Berkeley in 1976 with a degree in English Literature, she eventually became an elementary school teacher in Pittsburg, California, where she enjoyed a 25-year teaching career. In February 2013, she received an honorable mention for a poem she submitted to the Benicia Love Poetry Contest. She is also hoping to travel to Japan, believing strongly that in another life she was a Japanese haiku poet!

Spring

Life goes on, doesn't it?
The seasons change and continue on.
People are born, fall in love, live hopeful lives,
and fear a death they can't escape.
How many poems and songs have been written
about this never-ending cycle?
Even the children understand that a seed grows
into a glorious flower, exploding open,
only to fall apart and dry up...the seeds
swept away by late October.

Well, spring is here again and everyone
is finally waking up and stretching after
a long, sleepy hibernation.
People are running around
for the first time in months, or cruising
the streets in sleek, shiny convertibles,
feeling the sunlight bouncing off their heads.

My front yard is exceptionally beautiful this year.
The brilliant pink azaleas pop out around the
trunk of the Japanese maple.
The weeping cherry tree's long, bending branches
sway gently in the breeze, a soft waterfall of delicate,
paper-thin petals drifting to the ground.
People actually stop and sigh
as they walk past my yard.
And of course, I am delighted.

But inside my house, there is no spring.
Inside it is shadowed and cool,
like the beginning of autumn.
I watch you sit in a chair or look out the window,
gazing at the loveliness outside.

Johanna Ely

Having become the distant observer, you know that
none of this can really touch you.
You are experiencing a different kind of season…
The cancer inside you growing into a large, ugly, bulbous tumor,
oozing colors of blood red, pus yellow.
These are not the colors of spring, this is not
the way it is supposed to be.

And so we sit inside the house all afternoon, indifferent to
the beauty outside. We sit inside where it is
quiet and peaceful, listening to jazz on the radio
and reading poetry. Your eyes flutter open, then close.
For a while, even your pain is silent.
I decide to ignore the seasons and cycles…
What is important now is to forget everything but this,
To stay safe and protected in this moment, so that
I can read you another poem in the lingering light.

Johanna Ely

July Morning

The day flutters open
like an exhausted pale moth struggling for life.
Its wings too weak, almost lifeless,
become a flat slate sky, settling on my backyard,
endless and oppressive.
The morning light is cold, filtered,
its varying shades of light and dark grey
filling in the space between trees,
the chilly breezes turning the green oleander leaves
dry, yellow,
the hydrangeas fading early
into muted lavenders and browns.
Even the tomatoes are smaller this year.
Void of sun and heat,
they remain hard and round,
the size of large orange marbles.
I stay inside all morning
wearing pajamas and a fleece robe.
Looking for a tear in the drab wings,
streaks of blue light showing.

Retirement

The afternoon is a Monet blue,
a Renoir red,
a Chagall green.
The clouds are flying south with the geese
and the August sky dazzles me.
I sit in my backyard eating a turkey sandwich,
watching the trees sway,
listening to the leaves make their own music.
It is great to be alive I think,
to not work anymore, just relax,
and watch the day fold in on itself.
I still have time to
inhale, exhale,
inhale, exhale,
to breathe in a whole new life.

Joel Fallon

Poet Laureate Joel Fallon, Benicia's first (November '05 through July '08), is a retired Army officer who enjoys sailing, chess, gardening, and T'ai Chi. He graduated from the University of the Philippines in 1956. A trained Russian and Chinese linguist, Fallon served in Korea, Japan, the Philippines, and Germany. He retired after serving in the Pentagon with the Organization of the Joint Chiefs of Staff. His poems appear in several anthologies: the *Carquinez Poetry Review*, *Mijusiin* (The New Poetic Waves published by the Korean Poets Society of the Americas), *North Coast Literary Review*, the *Street Spirit*, and *POETALK*.

Moving Parts

So many moving parts: wife, kids, dog,
two cats, grand kids, cops, restraining orders,
diabetes, bad liver ...
It's hard to deal with so many moving parts.
Takes so long to turn the compost;
what good is compost anyway if I'm too busy
to fold it into my raised bed or spread it on my lawn?
I know how to fix the window but lack the time and juice.

Panjabi doctor shows me X-rays of my bunged up foot.
She says, "Look at all these signs of arthritis,
bone spurs and chips.
See the deformed bones?"

I thank her anyhow, "Shukria ganivad" in kindergarten
Hindi.
She smiles and prepares to say more but
I've heard enough
about my moving parts.

Twilight at the Asian Art Museum

Landscapes from a dream -
Crisp and clean and cool.
Calligraphy with brushstrokes
still vigorous after centuries.

Behind locked night doors
Buddha teaches compassion.
Shoji screen whispers shut,
rustle of silk robe and far away -
a flute.

Property Disposal

The funeral is all arranged.
No ritual is expected. Most of our stuff
is spoken for. We're comfortable with that.

Books, pictures and furniture all have destinations.
The silver? Perhaps they'll draw straws.
We hate to break up the set.

A youngster asks, "Grandpa, when will I get your sword?"
I tell him, "Pretty soon now,
pretty soon."

Paperboys Know

Paperboys know the feeling of getting it done
in the cold dimness - while smells are sharp
and it is quiet and the rest of the world is still in bed
reluctant to get up and take a leak.

Second Job

First light in the East -
Rooster, having done his job,
turns his thoughts to love -
his second job.

Don Peery

Don Peery of Benicia via Redding, California, has pursued an avocation of writing poetry for the past forty-five years. Don says, "I've experienced two marriages, four children, at least seven dogs, a couple of cats and four or five careers—but who's counting." Now in retirement, he is free to write, travel and enjoy life—"not necessarily in that order."

Wild Geese

  Late
    in fall's
      decaying hour,
        from vaulted V's descends their call
          to echo deep in mountain cleft -
            astride bold drafts of icy air,
              pressed on by cold's pursuing steed,
              they heed, those winged legions there,
            an ancient migrant call to flight,
          fleeing south to warming climes
        to feed and mark the ebb of time
      with wild yet patient
    beating
heart.

Winter Almond

Got a little anxious, didn't you?
Fickle winter sent a string of days
warm as any spring days are
and right away you decided it was time.

So you pooched your pink-white blossoms out
and scented up the air
inviting all the neighbor bees to sup
upon your table's fare.

Now look at you, your branches bare,
having cast your blossoms down to lie
strewn upon the icy breast
of earth's late-winter snow-white dress.

Summer Storm

Last night
I heard from an old friend -
a poem from out of my past
transmitted by wire
and electric pulse
from his mountain nest
to my valley home.

A summer storm crashed
behind his words,
echoing from the ridge
to the river and back,
lifting hairs
on the nape of my neck.

His voice was power,
speaking to me
of times past
when we were each
in grievous need
of the other.

Remembering,
I laughed for the phone
because I could not bear
that he should hear
tears flowing
quiet streams
from my eyes.

Don Peery

First Full Day of Fall

The first full day of fall is past -
night cools a leftover summer's blast.
The soil tilled in pre-noon's hour
lies quiet beneath a rising moon
as even night sounds fade, subdued,
anticipating autumn's power.

Already leaves begin their journey,
early dropped and walkway scattered,
yielding crisp crinkly sounds
to couples in their private passage.

Soon birds will start their annual run
to southern lands caressed by sun
much longer than these northern climes
wherein I sink my roots of time.

Yet comes winter, and with it snow
and gale driven December sleet -
but now is autumn poised to pause
to hold effect in check
while emphasizing cause....

Don Peery

Carol Smiles

An artist and writer of fiction, Carol Smiles counts poetry as a 'must do' activity to make life interesting and complete. She lives and writes in the Sacramento area. Look for her on Amazon and PublishAmerica online bookstores.

Tiny Tastes

Sweet tartness of lemon drops, bursts of ripe, reddened cherries,
   Touches of salt and pepper heat, find places on a tongue.
Scents of apricot, honeysuckle, jasmine and cinnamon,
   Float languidly past noses like melodies sung.
Eyes detect flashes and shapes, both familiar and rare,
   The segments of life's treasures, delicately rung.
How shall we view them? All sewn with silken stitches,
   Interwoven, intertwined, a tapestry created to be hung.
Within the silent hollows of the cavities in our souls,
   Let us marvel the versatility we've traveled among.
Blending them or relishing individually as they touch us,
   Cherishing before they disappear like snow-flakes flung.

Thanksgiving Prayer

We, as a people, have set aside one day to say Thank you
  For those things that have meant so much to each of us inside.
Individually we shut our eyes to dwell on what has been
  Most important, really special, those things we so often hide.
The things that make our world's spin stay on a level
  And comfort us along life's bumpy ride.
Perhaps to others they seem small in the general scheme of things,
  But to our merry-go-round they are the grease that make things glide.
A smile from a neighbor, a surprise gift or hand-clasp,
  A friendly grin and wave, a sympathetic ear in which to confide.
These are the things that are special when nothing else goes right.
  We've set this one day to represent all that is inside.
Saying Thanks in our hearts, for friends and their willingness to help
  When deep within us we feel the need for other voices to guide.
So here we are, gathered round a table or alone
  Saying from our depths a Thank you to those with which we abide.

Carol Smiles

Grief's Way

Healing is slow and follows a pattern
  Much like all in life.
We wait it out with quivering lips.
  Determination soothes the strife.
Getting through it is what we were always about...Together…...but now we're not.
Holding hands we marched in step
  As if to Drum and Fife.
This time when sunny days are reached,
  Laughter down the middle will be cut by a knife.
Though apart now, we seem still joined because we loved a lot.

Dark House

Our house is all but empty now, my loved one's left too soon.
I feel such loss, only a sliver remains of the moon.
But it has been promised that day will follow night. The sun shall shine on this ruin.
It will remind me of the laughter that was like bird song, bright and uplifting as noon.

John Goory

John Goory reaches into his mind, into the universe and his handmade and decorated Tarot cards to divine the unexplainable, to define one's needs and desires. From Chicago to Los Angeles to Benicia via Mill Valley and Santa Rosa, he is searching for the techno-pagan well-versed in PhotoShop while serving as the Director of Cinnabar—the Crystalline Center of Infinite Possibilities. He hopes for a publisher of his Tarot deck.

Somewhere in the Middle of Nature

Somewhere in the middle of nature
With heavy rain, fog, snow,
And raging wind
The world tree exists.
A god is tied to the tree
Upside down
He hangs there seemingly forever
Being tortured by the elements
Along with all the other gods
To torture his mind
He peers into the darkness
Perceiving a black mirror
The mirror is activated
It becomes even colder
Inside the mirror, he sees himself
In many different worlds and dimensions
At the bottom of the tree
He sees twenty-five different ruins
He grabs them feels well-being
And wisdom, too.
Then he becomes dizzy
And fainting
Falls to earth
With the twenty-five ruins as his guide
He was led
Word by word, idea by idea
Through his whole existence.
One into one   One into one   One into one
One becomes one

John Goory

Flow

A fertility source
An ankh which symbolizes the male and female
Energy to create the beginning
From the dark chaos
Down to the goddess to form the energy
Into matter
The ten-pointed star to show
The completion of the act
Then flowing down to the four elements
That form the high priestess
Who absorbs the elements
That create our universe
Which allows the consciousness
Of the human race to flow
Filling and racing like a tsunami
Clearing all before it
To cause a mutation as large as
Neanderthals to homo sapiens
So the human race can evolve
And join the rest of creation
On equal footing
With the universal mind.

Yah/Yum

The creation
Once humanity was one unit
    TAO
Like a whole peach
  However the peach
  Was split in half
  By whatever forces you believe in
  Resulting in the illusion
  Of duality.

  One half became the yang (male)
    The half with the pit

  One half became yin (female)
    The half with the empty space

Duality is illusion
Created by the split peach

It is what things are now
But no one is happy with it

To be whole again
The illusion must be recognized
And put back together

Like a solar eclipse
At its highest point

Or a five- and six-pointed star
Fused together by the
Japanese symbol for the mystic
Vibration of love
Back to the TAO
Back to peace.

Genea S. Brice

Poet, author, performer, and teacher, Genea Brice was raised in Vallejo, California. After graduating from Hogan High School and earning both a BA in English Literature and master's degree in Biblical Studies, she began honing valuable public speaking skills through classroom teaching and in local politics. Genea hopes to one day parlay her education, experience, and exposure into becoming Vallejo's first poet laureate.

The Waltz of the Autumn Mime

...Brown hand in Autumn's grasp...
Fingers spread out wide...
With veins and color and pointy tips
...looking a lot like mine...
The winds, the rains, those angry winds have all taken their course...
Replacing the lively, verdant thing; uprooting it from its source...
'Twas beautiful then...parading the prism, its strength and supple ways...
'Tis beautiful now...living out its last and solemn days...
Silent no more when crushed beneath the careless feet of men,
Subjecting, Rejecting, Neglecting such beauty is, to Nature, a sin...
So, glance again at the leaf that patiently bides the time,
...Prance again, Dance again...The Waltz of the Autumn Mime...

Geometry

It was geometry...
The angle of his shoulder, the line of his jaw...
To say nothing of the points of intersection...
Parallel, Perpendicular, Perfectly Spectacular...
...Thank you, Pythagoras, but my theory is: the shortest distance between two points is...breath...

Catharsis

Unapologetic Streams; liquid remorse…
Unsympathetic Screams; taking their course…
Little warm rivers spilling over the …DAM!
Deceiving façade, visage, and smile…
…Seeping now from the depths of the soul…weeping now…too late to console…
Infinite waters; humanity's cry…The number of stars that occupy the sky…Tally the sands that cover the sea…
Slow, Saline Tributary…
…Unapologetic Streams; liquid remorse…Unsympathetic Screams; taking their course…
                              Catharsis

My Father Died Today

My father died today…Just like they said he would…
…Perhaps when we lack internal prohibitions, external ones preside…
My father died today. I thought he never could…
…Perhaps when we seek eternal salvation, temporary substitutions never quite suffice…
My father died today. The dying was easy…it was the living that requires explanation…

Sherry Sheehan

Born and raised in Hawaii, Sherry Sheehan was a Las Vegas school psychologist before retiring to Crockett. Appointed poet laureate in 2006 for Ed Dewke's psoriasis website "FlakeHQ.com", she published *PoArtry* with artist Mary Reusch and *Across Currents* with artist Robert Chapla; participated in ekphrasticexhibits in Crockett, Danville, Fairfield, Livermore, Martinez, and Rush Ranch in California, as well as in Indiana and Michigan; and is happy to have had poems in every anthology of the Benicia *First Tuesday poets*, all five issues of *Carquinez Poetry Review*, and the last five "Ina Coolbrith Circle" Gatherings. Websites: google.com/site/sherrysheehanpoems/ and poetrymatters.150m.com/index_files/pages_files/sheehan.html

A Beaded Line

Rain fell before I awoke,
before I poured water
into the coffee-maker
and looked up to see a row
of birds, beading a power line,

each wet head of bird thought
an interior I imagined
as swarming with protozoa
like the drops of water
we studied in high school,

our heads bent over
microscopes while our
teen brains teemed
with what wasn't
in front of us,

distractions forming
that kept us from staying
focused on what was near,
as near as the wire of birds
I had noticed, now dispersed.

These birds had seemed
as settled and sure
as a single, uninterrupted thought
until my morning brew
permeated the darting place
between my ears,
and a new batch of birds
arrived on the wire
to replace the confluence
that had disappeared.

Sherry Sheehan

Attending

When I tune out on a subject,
important as it is to others
in the watching world,

when I'm overwhelmed by
bloodshed, brutality, riots,
revolutions, and rebellions
brought to my screen
by PBS, CNN, or the BBC,

and when I'm stupefied
by pundits' puzzling motives,
outcomes, and what-to-do's,

my hand grabs the remote,
my finger presses mute, ... and ...
all is stilled, letting me claim
what I can of calmness

until the next day,
when habit has me
again mired
in the news,
and I snap to,
trying to decide
whether I'm obliged
to know everything that TV
and computer screen
bring me,
wired and unwired,
and whether
attention to the tension
and attending 'til the ending
are required.

Sherry Sheehan

Tsundoku

Too many books,
newspapers, and magazines,
purchased or subscribed to
that one day very soon
I intend to read or reread,
have a name in Japanese:
tsundoku.

Neatly filed on living room shelves,
spread out on kitchen table and chairs,
lying beside the bed, or piled behind a door,
these objects taunt me.

Will I get to them when not grabbed
by the latest fad
on the screen of my desktop or iPad?

Not if the genes that I deplore
compel me to ignore
reams of print
already paid for
while I shop at a digital store
for more.

Sherry Sheehan

Jady Montgomery

Jady Montgomery discovered the Benicia First Tuesday Poetry Group in 2010, upon returning to northern California for the third time, to be near her daughter and new grandson. A granddaughter followed in 2013. About the practice of poetry, Jady says, "I'm forever grateful to my first teacher, Bay Area poet Ed Smallfield—and indebted to all teachers, mentors and fellow poets since—whose support and feedback encourage me to continue and begin anew, time and again. I find the effort to craft a poem the best way to make sense of our complex lives, histories, days, moments -- the blessings and challenges of consciousness."

Adaptation

The tiger will soon be extinct,
in my lifetime, experts say. No room
for all of us, all of us, all of us –
and the tiger too.

At noon today the downtown is teeming.
We weave through each other like flocks
flying close without touching.
Meanwhile, pigeons perch above
They thrive on high-rise ledges.
In our parks, their pearl grey heads
always bobbing just a breadcrumb away.
They warble, coo and thrum
in all dialects and tongues.

These most common, known also as the
Homing One. First called the Rock Dove,
but its cousins too – the White-Crowned,
the Wompoo, the Scaled and Pale-Vented,
the Short Billed and the ones called doves –
Ruddy Ground, White-Tipped, Doleful,
Diamond, and for love, the Turtle Dove.

They watch me below. I watch too.
All these people I'm walking through –
rainbow hues from pale sunrise to
deep-in-the-earth tones, over bones
thin as willow sprigs or thick as old oaks.
Faces in every third-grade shape.
Eyes speckled gold or mountain-lake blue,
rich-tar black, or flat green like the sea,
like mine, scanning now this rolling wave,
another sea, endless variety. It so satisfies.

I forget the tiger. She'll find no habitat
in our midst, will soon live only in my
television, where I'll watch, enlivened by
the sight of life reduced to raw essentials.
Hungry locomotive lunging at warp speed.
Then, the hunt over, she'll rest.
Tail weaving slowly in the hot air.
Warm blood on the muzzles of well fed cubs.

Jady Montgomery

Swimming Pool Blue

Why are swimming pools blue
when the bottoms are impossibly white,
bright as an endless day
at height of summer?

Pools reflect what's in the air, they say.
Blue sky is an illusion.
There's only blackness there
behind the light
refracting off the atmosphere
making emptiness of space,
the endless void,
appear to be a blue cocoon.

Our thoughts, the same,
an ether we emit,
our own cocoon
It bends and skews
the world, our days,
what it is
we think
we see,
not at all Reality.

Jady Montgomery

Falling In

You tell me that life as we know it will end
when we go over the fiscal cliff, that GMOs,
pollutants and pesticides are wreaking havoc
on our insides, that the hole in the ozone
is still growing, the polar caps going away.

These things are significant, I know.
So much that is so important – all this evidence
seeming to show how our time is already over.

But I am in another world where what I hold
in my arms has the power
to stop the clock and expand time all at once.

It's dawn. My grandson's head appears
around the guestroom door. Into the bed he climbs,
we cozy up, his feet tucked under my still sturdy legs.

We read a book or two of his choosing,
share laughs like chums
despite sixty years yawning between us.

Even before tomorrow,
he will remember nothing of this moment,
while my every cell will feed
on the unutterable gift of it
– for however long I have left on this earth –
breaking me open for the umpteenth time,
trying again to tell me something
I already knew but forgot.

Falling in love is like that.
Falling into life is like that.

Jady Montgomery

Deborah L. Fruchey

Deborah Fruchey attempted to write her first book at 8 years of age. She is the author of two comedy romance novels and one self-help manual, *Is There Room for Me, Too? 12 Steps and 12 Strategies for Coping with Mental Illness*. Her first formal collection of poetry, *Armadillo*, will be released in 2014. You can find more of her work at www.lastlaughproductions.net, or visit her at www.lafruche.net.

Facing Things

I value my wrinkles as conversation pieces.
When I was young, with flawless skin,
my face said, I have experienced nothing.
I am exciting to have sex with.
I will misunderstand and judge you.
I have the sympathy of a rock.
As you can see, I've never faced
a thing.

No more bikinis now. My skin doesn't fall
into the public domain any more.
Noticed by the few, my face says

Talk to me.
I have lived with pain.
I have stories to tell.
I have made mistakes.
I know about longing for things
and waiting
and giving up longing
swallowing life's bitter coffee each morning
unsweetened by ignorance.
My life has slowed down.
I have time to listen.

Why would I pay to be restored
to a bland and blinding smile?
And as for sex,
my principal organ
has always been
the brain.

Deborah L. Fruchey

The Writer's Nightmare

In this one, the place is all corridors.
No doors or exits, mind you – only corridors.
Construe.
Flaking stucco, skeletons, and babies.
Not just any babies.
My babies.
Miniature birdlike bones of books I never wrote.

In penance I wander those halls.
The manuscript babies limp by without seeing me
crippled, amputated, deformed
some without bodies and some without voice
the ashes of serious novels making
dirty rugs of arcane pattern
the cut-off laugh of comedy ghosts
lifting my hair
like the damp touch of fungus.

The end of the dream, I presume,
is that I hack my way out with my children behind me
set fire to the office and chop up the kitchen
flush down the toilet
my boyfriend, my bills, the laundry basket
the car, the dishes, the telephone
the appointment book.
Then the babies and I throw a party to which
no one else in the world is invited.

But I really can't say if that happens for sure.
In real life, each morning I wake up too soon.
I wake to the sound of a desperate wailing.
They tell me this is only
the alarm clock.

Deborah L. Fruchey

Waiting Room

She listens
perched on a crackling sheet of paper
white as Chinese mourning
which they will throw out
without writing or drawing on it
or wrapping up
any other meat.

She sits
unbutchered as yet
white cotton robe dropped
on a plastic chair
shielded in the many-shaded monotony
of the clothes she came in with
a purse clasped in her lap
full of graphic brochures.

She looks
for a bland white door
to open
for a scribbled tablet
to tear
for a scrubbed white shirt
to tell her
what color tomorrow will be.

Deborah L. Fruchey

Linda R. Toby

Linda Toby is a California native presently living in Benicia, California. Past residences include living in the mountains, and by the sea. Education includes a bachelor's degree in Nursing with a secondary vocation of Holistic Health Care Practitioner. Interests include: writing poetry, travel, hiking, and navigating life's unpredictable path.

Faith is Fickle

In the deepest troughs, I peer upwards
Towards the pastel blue sky wishing for the unseen
To lift me from my most recent quagmire.
In recession, faith builds to strengthen my resolve
To change, morph, and redefine how to rise from the ashes.

Blackened by soot,
Improvement comes when ashes
Blow away in the breeze,
When the grey slate clears.

Fickleness, my true nature with faith,
Doubts its existence during the peaks,
The days of triumph.
Rapidly memory fades.
Gratefulness disappears into twilight.

Too much invested effort
In celebration and elevated ego
Obscures my view.
Fickleness is how I tumble into darkness,
Stubbing my toes along the way.

Linda R. Toby

Fade into Green

Fade into green
Greed and more mouths to feed

Life unchanged with seasons
Tossed like silver coins in a slot machine,
Clocks tick in bold cadence
Toward our future.

Man's hungry green eyes altered these
Sacred cycles of time.

Fade into green
Greed and more mouths to feed

Above the brick and mortar of faltered
Wall Street, a pale anaemic blue sky expands
To all corners of the earth. Across the universe
From the cold cavernous moon, our world
Radiates hues of aqua blue, nebulous white,
Forest green and brown-red coloured bursts.

Earth once plentiful, now

Fades into Wall Street greed
With more mouths to feed

Seasons cascade towards an unknown fate
Will primitive green-backs prevail, or will
Ageless blue ocean and sky,
White clouds of rain and snow,
And bronze earth burgeoning with new seed
Soothe destiny's wait?

Greed and more mouths to feed
Fade into green

Linda R. Toby

Hillside of Silent Souls

Gazing out a side window
Viewing rolling green hillsides
Recede to silent soldier saluting centaurs,
White marbled stones crowd together
Like high rises to the alabaster sky.

Deceased slammed unceremoniously together,
Inches from one another
Mirror a vibrant pulsating city
In the distant obsidian skyline.

Predecessors rest their heads on a hillside of silent souls,
As swaths of fluorescent green
Brush adjacent to artery clogging stone,
Reflecting those who have been,
Those who are now living, and
Those who will join the masses on Halloween.

Linda R. Toby

Bonnie Weidel

Bonnie Weidel was a student of Theodore Roethke and Stanley Kunitz at the University of Washington, Seattle. Bonnie earned her BA following completion of a thesis on the poetry of Wallace Stevens. As a single mom, she returned to the University of California at Berkeley as a Master's candidate in Studio Art followed by graduate work in arts education, earning a secondary teaching credential. This was in turn followed by an AA from Solano Community College and an MA from Sonoma State University in Early Childhood Education. As director of Benicia's Art For Kids, she curates exhibits and presents workshops on visual arts education. For twenty-four years, she served as Benicia Community Arts president and founder, coordinating the annual Festival of Arts in the Park. In addition, Bonnie coordinated Christmas at the Clocktower for ten years, with emphasis on Benicia cultural history and traditional crafts; served 10 years on the Library Gallery Advisory Committee, and currently coordinates an exhibit of Children's Art at various locations emphasizing the child's cognitive development and the exhibit of craft and trades for the Historical Museum.

Sometimes The Wind

Sometimes the wind
speaks like my friend---
intonations without end

Other times it howls
a moaning soul
excluded by my bedroom wall

Sometimes it plays
in fallen leaves
sifting, sorting, as it please,

Sometimes in covert silence tries
to make me think
it isn't there.

How is it words
in transit are
a windy passion to explore,

touching corner, cave and spire?
Whence motivated, why and where,
without a wall or boundary

who can describe the windy ride
of the wind within
and wind outside?

Bonnie Weidel

The Course of Poetry

I thought of poets as
Greek gods, Trojan warriors,
Assyrian kings, brave cosmonauts--
And not like us,
the teacher, clerk or pastry server,
such as we know are poets now.

They must have been great kings,
I thought, those poets, their great souls
not TV nurtured, intravenous fed,
reading all the readings they could read,
unburdened by thoughts
of nukes and radiation,
global warming and the like.

I thought they were
unlike today, in birth and vigor,
death, demise.
But words equivocate and as
we talk of love and war
we hear the echo in our voices,
a cadence of the marching, singing mind
that could sustain
the night, the morning light and
night again.

Bonnie Weidel

On Self-Sufficiency

too busy living
to re-live my life
too pressed for time
to call a friend
I watch the sky
like a cactus in the desert
issues and answers
piling high

Who needs it anyway?
An easy breath, a lazy song?
A gift to toss, a book to browse.
Who knows how many have begun
standing on the bottom rung
alone in all this numbered night
the stars we do not see
or zone
a murmur on the microphone?

Oh, sing, before there's none to hear
and dance
before the music stops--
a feather spinning on the ice,
the ace card and a roll of dice.

Bonnie Weidel

Robert Shelby

Robert Shelby says: "Little of my life has been at all poetic. Through it so far, I've struggled to write finely crafted poems, good poems both informative and entertaining. Few have any idea how much I wrote in six decades or how much I still write. I had good teachers, starting with my parents. Major publication still awaits though numerous poems have seen print and I've self-published several books."

Sorcery In Stress

A vice squeezes you
as between jaws and poems
flow out like leaven.
Thus from hard steel is heart flesh
pressed madly into flowers.

Ah, Nameless Love, Unending Romance

Be wild, my heart, flame in the wind,
There will be time enough for peace
When with the stones you condescend
To lay me in the earth and cease.

Be hifalutin' in the summertime.
Dance and be carefree through the fall.
There will be leaves enough to rhyme
When spring's bird grows too gruff to call.

Be sure, my mind, to make good sense
And play my syntax as you pay
For all my licensed verses dense
With arsis, thesis and decay.

Ferment, my soul, a heady wine,
There will be time for threnody
When I am walled around with pine
In dignified serenity.

Robert Shelby

On Sylvan Mountainside

A ripple dappling
sunlight shines on embankment
  above the creek pool . . .

Sky glow on the pool
reflects down-grown pine forest
waving gentle wind . . .

Up-grown pine forest
darkly above pooled sky glow
shadows frothing falls . . .

Robert Shelby

Musing On The Sphere

At the still center of the turning earth, gravity is nil.
In the central flux of political life, individuals weigh little.
"Heavyweights" are they who endure the crowded buffeting
of diverse opinion. At earth's weightless point, mass
lacks centrifugal impulse. So in secure seats of government
no one wants out. "Lightweights" participate in crowding.
What of stations midlife in middle earth? Far from surface
events in the deep churning world nearer center than suburbs,
men feel floating urges to escape, but they stay trapped
by weight of lighter people as surely as, beneath earth's
mantle, super dense metal finds no escape
through massively in-crowding, lighter rock.

A president fibrillates in everyone's desires. Having reached
his pinnacle, has he still his own goals? He may imagine them.
He may work tirelessly to lead peripheral events that turn
him around. Information and directives must be manhandled, his
feelings whirl with no means of expression but to stay in order
while bold fiats and fine programs fountain out to trickle
on recalcitrant desert. Earth rotation and revolution are complicated
by common center with the moon, at odds with mere geometry,

churning the deep interior while in turn both find their true center
with the sun which flies around the galaxy. So, too, the states
and nation complicate a world where everyone feels central to
self and every self partially identifies with some composite.
What is it like inside stars? Such fusion and effusion, fission and
revision---the greatest star a gnat-feast to occasional dark brilliance
of a universe when all mass reunites in a space smaller than
a schoolboy's penciled period where baryons bang
togetherness apart and recreate Time's arrows. Repercussion
like no cherry bomb must so punctuate phrases of cosmic silence
that if we realize the center of our being, we no longer fear
trivialities like interstellar distance or local noise, nor mind
that we are viscous smoke destined to dissipate,
for there will be no loss, nor shall we miss a thing.

Robert Shelby

Frances Jackson

Frances Jackson is a native Californian. Her first poetic efforts began and ended at age seven, when a skeptical teacher said she could not have written that poem (a rhyming trifle about Christopher Columbus). Decades passed in other pursuits before she heard of the Benicia First Tuesday Poets. In 2008, with three new poems in hand she landed on safe poetic ground in the company of Poet Laureate Robert Shelby and his kind fellows. She has written and self-published a small historical Western novel and is working on a sequel.

Date Rape

Smile nor ease betray him
though her quickened heartbeat may've
for she has longings too
but wisdom yet to form
so she enters chaste
the darkened car's embrace

A wedge of moon that night
did not fully hide the sight
of an ancient inequality
while gentler people slept
the weakest of them wept
her wounds too deep to bind

Now see her splintered hope
how he completely ruined it
how from her fingers to her toes
a muted madness flows
and every tender thing he touched
has folded into stone

Carmel

On finest sands of pearl white
for worn out toes and paws alike
we descend this steep way down
that leads to Miracle Mile

To north and south, an endless shore
that sends its foam in scalloped forms
and sunlight at horizon's edge
a silver sheet that stuns the eye

Coolest green the curling waves
that find a gentle way to gauge
their force on little nine pound Poms
who chase their balls into its arms

It gently sends them back to shore
like little surfers who mistake
uncaring seas for benign joy
harmlessly void of treachery

We came from this same scalloped foam
to climb the sand we just have combed
in endless legions of our like
to build the cities and the lights

We'd watched so long through watery eyes
'til heat and webbed hands reached to ground
surfing from the aqua dream
into a harsh awakening

We mind for hours what God hath wrought
in heaven's supreme cosmic thought
and steep our souls in living source
astonished - at our salty tears.

Frances Jackson

Yuba Site 5 & 7
(Inspired by the paintings of Linda Grebmeier)

I hazard the spectre
of faces in the window
step around
the gleaming cross laid down
on pooled, red ground.

only afraid
of who women fear
in abandoned spaces
discarded places
where no one hears
you weep.

light plunges through
the broken roof
like crash of lightning
rays of morning
potential energy
in empty dawning.

abandoned now
the cavernous rooms
where busy workers milled
beneath the shattered palisade
that rusty beams still span

along steel ruins
resound the groans
which seem to speak with scorn,
"flesh can't be forged
nor spirit formed
to mend my broken bones."

Frances Jackson

Bobbie C. Richardson

Poet, radical, patriot, Bobbie Richardson is also the seventh child of the seventh child born on the seventh month, in Monroeville, Alabama. He notes this city gave us Harper Lee, author of To Kill a Mockingbird; Truman Capote, author of In Cold Blood; Marva Collins, renowned African American educator; and John Drew of the Atlanta Hawks. Married with three girls and two boys, Bobbie lists writing poetry and singing among his hobbies. His heroes are Senator Bernie Sanders of Vermont, Michael Jackson, Jessie Owens, Nelson Mandela, Michael Moore, Jessie Jackson Sr., Martin Luther King Jr., Maya Angelou, journalist Helen Thomas, and Bill Maher. Bobbie says, "I get most of my news from Aljazeera America, Benicia Patch and the local news outlets. I am a card-carrying member of Moveon.org, NAACP, and Barry Scheck's Innocence Project."

99 Percenters Had Enough!!!

We've heard all your lies
Had Enough!
Your pathetic Alibis
Had Enough!
Your selfish "pie in the sky"
Had Enough!
You took us for a fool
Shame on you!
You're just a lying tool
You'll get your due!
We should have seen the Game
Shame on us.
Our Patriotism was all in vain
We're bout to bust
But now we are all aware
Had enough!
Our trust is small but there
Had Enough!
Now we demand LAISSEZ FAIRE
HAD ENOUGH!
HAD ENOUGH!!
HAD ENOUGH!!!

The Revolution Will Not Be Televised (re-visited)

You will not be able to stay home Brothers and Sisters. You will not be able to plug in, turn on and cop out. You will not be able to lose yourself in thought and slip; slip out for a beer during commercials. Because the Revolution will not be televised. The Revolution will not be televised. The Revolution will not be brought to you by The Apple iphone 5, 6, 7, 8, 9 and 10 without commercial interruptions. The Revolution will not show you pictures of Obama blowing a bugle like Gabriel, and leading a charge by Reverend Wright, General Petraeus and John Kerry, to eat fried chicken confiscated from a Chicago Sanctuary. The Revolution will not be televised. The Revolution will not be brought to you by C.N.N. or Aljazeera America and will not star Nicole Kidman or Morgan Freeman or Wolverine or The Incredible Hulk. The Revolution will not inject collagen in your lips to Africanize them and give them sex appeal. The Revolution will not curl your hair to make it look more ethnic. The Revolution will not inject collagen in your butt to make it more Africanized and plumper and firmer and sexier; because the Revolution won't care. There will be no YouTube of you and Rodney King pushing that shopping cart down the block to a dead end street or trying to slide that color television into a stolen car. Fox News will not be able to predict another winner at 8:30 or report from 29 Districts and have it un-constitutionally approved by the U.S. Supreme Court. The Revolution will not be televised. There will be no YouTube of neighborhood Security Guards shooting down unarmed young Black men in the instant replay. There will be no YouTube of cops shooting down unarmed young Black and Brown men in the instant replay. There will be no YouTube of Whitney Houston singing "I will always love you" and there will be no YouTube of The Reverend Al Sharpton strolling through D.C. in a Red, Black and Green liberation jumpsuit that he had been saving for just, "Such and Such an occasion." Reality TV will no longer be so damned relevant, and women will not care if Oprah or any of the new female talk show hostess keep bashing Heterosexual men; because Black people will be too busy in the streets looking for a better day. The Revolution will not be televised. There will be no highlights on the Eleven O'clock news and no YouTube of female liberationists protesting and screaming, "Keep your laws off our bodies." The theme song will not be written by Burt Bacharach, nor rapped by Kanye West or Gil Scott Heron, himself. The Revolution will not be televised. The Revolution will not be right back after a few messages about a "black horse, black ice, or black people." You will not have to worry about a chicken in every pot, a bail out for your bank, Wall Street being too big to fail or a Government shutdown. The Revolution will not be bottled like God given free water and sold for a profit. The Revolution will not fight foreign Wars on Foreign Lands only to come back home to be drafted in Zuckerberg's Plan. When its' all said and done The Revolution will indoctrinate you; Because The Revolution
Will not be Televised!
Will not be Televised!!
Will not be Televised!!!

Fairfield...There's No Fare There!

Fairfield
The County Mounty
Once I ran into Garamendi there
Was he collecting a Bounty
Don't do the crime
If you can't walk the time
And walking you will do
Alone with a date to see the Judge
Hours of miles will ensue
Kicking Rocks you will
in the good ole U.S. of A.
Cause you've been cited out,
You can't stay
Now getting home is a must
You'd think a TaxPayer
would get five dollars
for the Bus!!!
Ohhh!!! But not in Fairfield,
Where nobody cares!!
Yes they call it Fairfield
But why?
      There's no FARE There!!!

Bobbie C. Richardson

Michael R. Merris

Michael Merris was born Feb. 12, 1953, in Jacksonville, Illinois. He started writing in the 8th grade, started drinking at 13, and became an intermittent black-out drinker by age 15. He shipped as a merchant seaman for 2 years and then enlisted in the United States Navy. In the '80s, clean and sober, he moved to the SF Bay Area and has worked in internet technology for 30 years. He married late and was divorced after 15 years. He has 2 sons. Currently he is working on a book of stories titled *Waving Goodbye* and seeking a publisher for his second chapbook of poems, *Smoked Topaz*.

looking back

i screamed
my pain
for all
yet no one
asked
why I was so
hurt,
so mad.
i mumbled poems
that stopped men
short
sent their stares
burning into
vacancy
at my words
yet no one
asked
where
it came
from.
it wasn't until
my senior year
that my mother
finally asked
why I was so
hurt,
so mad.
it stopped me short
from mumbling cold porcelain porcelain
and I have been a coward
ever since.

Michael R. Merris

Craftsman

for Bill Gearhart in Heaven

he always claimed
Craftsman was the best.
always could get a replacement
free when broken.
told me how an X gave
ALL his tools away
even the ones his father gave him.
looked into his eyes and saw
a hollowness in his heart.
had to start from the beginning
once again
with Craftsman.

we worked swings
drooled over tool catalogues
went to Sears
to look around
at lunch.

didn't know
until later
the hollowness
of losing tools
a hollowness that can't be filled.

felt that hollow again
when I learned he passed.
one more lost
one more connection realized
too late;
Craftsman.

change

change is inevitable,
they say,
like rain
when you have to mow the grass,
but
sometimes something sticks
in granite boulders bracing the sea
that last forever,
maybe not that,
but long enough
like black top lines running into the sun.

Michael R. Merris

at 50

for Darren Glorioso who heard it first

at 50
you pray for no more than 15
20 at the outside
then the maggots
can mug
your rotting corpse
tempting you no longer
for something that simply wasn't
in the cards,
wasn't on your
path.
at 50
you think of
all the young dudes
who danced the night away and ended up
alone,
some for their own
doing
and for some
others.
at 50
your new shrink
looks you in the eye
and tells you that we die alone
and you hear in his voice The Jackal's grin
and you see in his voice an offering hand.
and you are grateful
and you reflex a laugh and wait the end.
at 50
people leave and join in for
the ride until their stop. True, some
stay and others are picked up from the past.
The ones who are true hold you until the end and
never ask a thank you and you
never ask why not?
at 50,
things seem not to matter
love surely doesn't
and these scars
your sins.

Michael R. Merris

Peter Bray

Peter Bray grew up in the 1950s in the suburbs of Walnut Creek, California, graduating from Las Lomas High School, Diablo Valley College and the University of California, Berkeley. He's worked as a design engineer, illustrator, graphics designer, supervisor, manager, and handyman. He has written poems for forty years and songs for twenty, and a weekly column, "The A Cappella Handyman," for the Benicia Herald since 2008. His efforts can be found on YouTube and Facebook. He publishes a free, monthly eclectic newsletter, "Taproot & Aniseweed." He's a member of the Benicia First Tuesday Poetry Group, the American Academy of Poets, and the Ina Coolbrith Poetry Circle.

Grief's a Hard River...

Grief's a hard river,
it'll maybe take you down,
bouncing along the bottom
and hoping that you don't drown.
Remembering their last moments
and all the memories before,
gotta go to work
and so it's hard to close that door.
I used to think that Harry
being a special cat,
knew something about being feral
and could link me somehow to Cat'.
But it's all too absurd,
knocking on Heaven's door,
all their artifacts are around,
but still I'm wanting more.
Grief's a hard, hard river.

I am a Weed...

I am a weed
in your corporate concrete.
I'm the stain
that won't go away.
The light to and from
that crack in the wall;
that writing on the wall
that you may not be able to read.
I'm the light in the tunnel
to somewhere.
Get used to me,
I'm gonna be around
for a long, long time.

Irrigation Ditch...

Here I am the empty and weed-choked
irrigation ditch, at the perimeter of a
field of dry thistle and dust,
full of potential but little else,
and you, you are a deep well of water,
clear and a small trickle at first,
but now you become deeper, colder;
a torrent of healing and refreshingly full –
a deep gorge, a wellspring of clear wonder.
I listen closely to your sound and feel
your pulsating turbulence –
Fill me deep and run through me,
together we will water the dry
and arid fields everywhere –
And things will do
what they're supposed to do
when deep water meets
an irrigation ditch,
they will GROW!

Peter Bray

Stepping Into Stony Creek/Grief Healing...

Stepping into Stony Creek, I'm 12 again,
the shallow ripples over creek pebbles
from fishing hole to fishing hole
are a steady comfort – It's summer-warm,
but not yet hot. My tennis shoes protect
my feet from intrusions but the water is cool
but not cold and runs over brownish-yellow,
but safe, creek algae. My brothers are not
so far away, my parents are back at the farm
doing what parents do, and the grandparents
are OK – I have no worries and no
serious aspirations. In minutes I can be asleep
if I carry on with this meditational serenity.
I am now 70 and I reach out for my daughter Cat',
pull her in close to me to aid in the Grief Healing
I'm trying to go through but will never recover from.
I hold her close to me and I fall asleep.
If this is as close as I can get to her in Heaven,
wherever that may be, I'll have to settle for that.

Juanita J. Martin

Juanita Martin, Fairfield's first poet laureate (2010-2012), is an award-winning poet, a freelance writer, and a performance artist. She's author of *The Lighthouse Beckons*, a collection of poems. Her book was accepted into several branches of the Solano County Library. Her poem "Emancipate Me" was accepted as a part of the Benicia Historical Museum's permanent exhibit "Freedom is a Hard Bought Thing," which commemorated the 150th anniversary of the Emancipation Proclamation. Her poetry appears in *Blue Collar Review, SoMa Literary Review, Rattlesnake Review*, and *Bay Area Poets Review*. She's active in Ina Coolbrith Circle, Redwood Writers, Marin Poetry Center, and Benicia First Tuesday Poets. She's been a featured reader at Healdsburg Literary Guild, Petaluma Poetry Walk, Healdsburg Literary Café, and the Berkeley Poetry Festival. Juanita is working on another book of poetry called *Quiet Intensity*. www.jmartinpoetwriter.com

Girl On The Water

she's a vision of silky white against satiny black
bony fingers and toes posed like a ballerina
her ghostly skin bathed in the canvas of the deep
her slender face brushed with wind-swept hair
as the silent sky watches
the moon frames her symmetry
casts an eerie reflection
her final dance on a watery stage

Silent Winter

A tree bowing, sighing,
Bending, breaking, limbs heavy,
Sap frozen in bark
Hiccups of powder fall
Bone cold rips at its core
A savior and a cypher, souls in peril,
An unforgiving blade takes a sacrifice
Man warms himself in the silent winter

Red-Tailed Hawk

Casual jaunt to Petaluma in the Cruiser,
The sky painted ocean blue
An early spring was upon me
A morsel or two later,
A red-tailed hawk swooped down
Caught by my windshield,
Caught by my eyes too late,
As feathers and metal were entwined
The hawk and I answered a call of nature
Two souls blinded by the sun,
Blinded by instinct
Collided on a path of survival

Juanita J. Martin

Pandora Bethea

Pandora Bethea was born in Athens, Greece, to a maternal Greek family of literary and performing artists and to an English engineer father working in Iran. She lived in Iran until she was ten, when the family moved back to Athens. Because she was surrounded by many languages, cultures and traditions, multiculturalism was her comfort zone. She first came to the US when she was twenty-six. Pandora is presently teaching high school English in Antioch, where she often discovers young poets in the classroom. She lives in panoramic Crockett, except for summers, where she can be found with her two grown children, Maya and Alex(ander), and their extended Greek family on an Aegean island. Her poetry has been published in "Healdsburg Haiku" by Running Wolf Press, in "The Peace Press" of Sonoma County, in "the Sitting Room" annual publication, and she has read her own and other poetry in the Morning Haiku radio program for KRCB Radio in the past. She writes poetry both in English and Greek, and loves being part of the poet community of the San Francisco Bay.

Food Stamps

Brown, White, Black, Yellow
that interwoven pattern of despair
on every face, whatever color.

Sitting on plastic chairs,
row after row of poverty.
Eyes staring down at dirty floors,
ears perched in case one's called,
one being a number, not a person.

The wall clock stretches its arms.
A stranger's voice calls out her name
as if from the depths of Hades.
She arises, unstable at first,
and steps up to the occasion.

Strip down to the bone
of how much, when, where, why.
When satisfied, the interrogator leads her
to another barren room.

And after she is classified,
demystified,
recorded,
photographed,
fingerprinted and
awarded,
she gathers the remnants of her fighting spirit
and returns home with food.

Feminist Love Poem

My heart is like a spinning wheel
spokes radiating through space
you've placed between us.

My heart is like a solid wheel,
circular planet rotating around
your darkened days and lightened nights.

My heart is like a Ferris wheel,
pleasure suspended in fear:
the dangers of a screaming joyride.

My heart is like a runaway wheel,
stumbling over winding, uneven roads,
those carved in your face of pain.

My heart is like Sisyphus's wheel,
hope rolling up a steep mountain,
knowing the leap of faith is inevitable.

My heart is like a wheelbarrow,
guts exposed, ready to carry meaning,
while it rests before the heavy load.

My heart is like a fortune wheel,
gambling with your needs, your smile, your words,
seeking victory over your cruel manipulation.

Can you be the axle that will rotate us in unison?
If not, let go of the steering wheel and I will drive
myself
home.

Pandora Bethea

My Daughter and I Will Fly

From one coast to another,
across the ancient land
together we will fly,
my daughter and I.

She has chosen the airline,
a symbol of freedom its logo.
Irony has it we miss our flight
and spend the morning imprisoned
in the gated airport
surrounded by artificial light.

Snapping like wild cats in a cage,
she with her raging PMS,
I with my mad menopause,
we battle over the nail file
and deliberately sharpen
our red pointed nails,
ready to blame each other
for our unbearable captivity.

But tomorrow we will march together,
her soft, smooth hand
in my rough, dry one,
her brisk, rebellious step
with my slow, determined one,
chanting our mantras for women's lives,
for freedom, for equality, for justice.
She with a voice loud and brave,
I with one deep and persistent,
Demeter and Persephone,
Pandora and Maya,

marching through the centuries,
nurturing the cosmos with our rich, sweet,
female milk,
giving unconditionally to our Great Family.

From one coast to another,
across the ancient land,
together we will fly,
my daughter and I.

Pandora Bethea

Colin Amato

Colin Amato was born in 1989 and raised in Benicia. He began writing short stories in middle school. In high school he discovered the beauty of poetry in Mr. Greenwood's Creative Writing Class. Thanks to his Mom and Dad, Colin has been exposed to many different authors and poets. He finds inspiration from the mystical poetry of Mevlana Celaleddin-i Rumi, The Beats, and Charles Bukowski. In the spring of 2013, he received his BA in Psychology at San Francisco State University. From studying Carl Jung, Colin feels poetry and other art forms connect us to the collective unconscious and thus unite all humans in a common form of unique expression. His poetry can be read at: http://www.poetrysoup.com/poems_poets/poems_by_poet.aspx?ID=15305

Poetic Occupation

As a poet I am told
I am a "maker" in Greek
I am a "seer" in Latin
taking words and plucking them
from the primordial void
plucking from the infinite fields
grazing in the tall lush grass
sucking on succulent peaches
in the golden brown sun

I take these words, images from
the Collective Unconscious Soup
and plug, upload them to the
constant iPod on playlist repeat
seeing the images which none
but myself can comprehend

I take those images
bringing them down
to the workshop
the smithy
the red-hot volcano
I set about to work
        to craft
to make these thoughts and
expressions tangible
understandable to all
set up and ingrained in
the senses of the mind
permeating from above and now
reflected and palatable to everyone

Colin Amato

Carrousel at Night

Crazing clown face rises
above the four-way road
chucking chunky Iron coins
down its comedic throat
roller-coaster amusement
carrousel at night
silently spinning
moving against the slight
wind, pushing everything
along its shy way

Cafe of Sorrow

Sitting, smiling, still
in the Cafe of Sorrow
Mom, Dad and Child
fine clothes, cradling on
close knee, protective
many in lively, livid
discussion, laughing, embracing
the moments that life
brings.

Out of chai, WTH?
Never mind my fair Italian
stud of a waiter
I'll have green tea
and an oatmeal cookie
the steam rises from
the lime-green moat
embraced by brown cup
and saucer   protective
old poet with notebook

and glass of wine, the
only two things he needs
shrill music rises above
our heads wrestling with the
various chattering and
the slamming of the
espresso machine. The
noise is its own orchestra
in this protective cave of
sorrow.

The red stockings various
names sewed in
hang from the ceiling a
holiday reminder to those
who already didn't know
the time of season

The music, now Italian
opera rises and so do
our souls with it. The
half-eaten cookie is eaten
tea is drunk, all wrestling
in my organs,   protective

in that tunnel of sorrow
get up and go, embrace the
day, leaving the protective
Cafe of Sorrow behind.

Anxiety

Feeling body is present
Mind ahead catch the other
My brain out of breath

Carole Dwinell

Carole Dwinell has been an artist/writer for as long as she can remember. She is convinced that there is much more in practice, practice, practice than in relying on "talent"—whatever that is. Art and poetry exist to distill the flood, to find a route of fire to burn a way into the heart of the observer, the one who is looking. And that's the hard part, finding the ones who are looking. www.caroledwinell.com

Sentinel

Eastward facing toward each morning's door
is Spider Woman, mesa framed, sentinel of stone.
Tall, alone, in Canyon de Chelly, an old rapport.

Made of sandstone, high above the canyon's floor
she's a weaver, casting up a spider's web alone
eastward facing toward each morning's door

she throws it up, and laced with dew, to explore
waning night, filled now with stars, loom grown.
Tall, alone, in Canyon de Chelly, an old rapport.

The stars share the dark with Diné early lore.
Coyote howls tales to the night with perfect tone
eastward facing toward each morning's door

All embracing spirits give directions in asking for
Nature to keep the People safe from Spider crone,
tall, alone, in Canyon de Chelly, an old rapport.

Diné do not speak of Spider Woman anymore
unless it's winter, then it's safe to quietly, alone
facing eastward toward each morning's door,
tell of her, in Canyon de Chelly, with old rapport.

Carole Dwinell

Golden

It is the moment electric,
the one with no borders,
when the golden eagle
sweeps across the sky.

Is it the hunt this time?
Or just a favorite updraft
to simply ride way high
then dive, catch it again.

A territory of many miles
to search, these lifelong
pairs, reflection mates,
occupying nest in shifts,

both caring for young.
Silence, as is their wont.
so swift and deadly, small
creatures must be mindful.

It is the moment electric,
the one with no borders,
when the golden eagle
sweeps across the sky.

a growl in the night

no one can hear that roar of the many who come surrounded with hunger
and cold, those we can't, don't wish to see, invisible, forgotten, a pointed
avoidance. we need weep for the desperate silent ones, the ones whose
starvation growls in the night, those whose unheard voices scream
for the quiet of purpose, whose tears become thunder at waste of lives.
The ones who languish in the shadows of tall concrete and glass towers,
discarded and consumed by yesterdays. What small thing will finally blossom
and quiet the deaf sound of this cancerous country's unborn future, a path
unrelenting which approaches through dark walls of despair, wails
that become avenging growls in the night ... that then will not be stilled.

Carole Dwinell

When the Heat Is On

No one told me that I was going to be inside a pot forever, again and again on the stove, always having to add new ingredients to keep something going, always simmering, steaming away ... giving off aromas, fumes, fragrant, enticing, repelling, toxic or otherwise while all this simmering, boiling, frying, burning, was going on. Temperature rising. There's no lid on it. No. Look. Get close. You can see the flavors of eagerness, desire, caring, fright, confidence, hate, love, not to mention the motion of cooking, a stir embracing you, a taste tempting you ... the feel of a heat that reaches out and cleverly pulls you right into the pot with no warning at all. A salacious cook top with all kinds of dials and knobs. Turn here to lower the temperature, here to increase the heat. Lets you think you are in control. Ha! Fooled you. It's a lie about a watched pot never boils. It seethes. Might be safer, though less interesting, to
... get out of the kitchen!

Jonathan Pasco, Sr.

Jonathan Pasco, Sr. is a native Benician who grew up in a setting that was right out of a Disney movie. He attended public and private schools and graduated from Benicia High School. He went to Solano College at night while working days. He worked a variety of jobs and even traveled up and down California with various carnivals. Now an avid online PC gamer, he continues to reside in Benicia as a single father of two kids. He has over twenty years as a union carpenter, is head bouncer at a local establishment, ran a martial arts school in town and is working toward his 3rd degree black belt. Past experiences have only fueled and inspired a passion for writing.

Invisible to You

I'm invisible to you
    I wander your streets but that's nothing new.
You say I'm lazy, I'm drunk and dangerous too
    But you know in your heart
        It just isn't true
It hurts not to eat
    I know about that
The least of my worries
    Is "getting too fat"

I'm invisible to you
    Can you imagine how it would be
Alone on the streets
    Robbed of all dignity

I almost died for my country
    In a foreign war
Now even the local supermarket
    Won't let me in the door

I'm invisible to you
    Is that how you want me to stay
Out of sight, out of mind
    I'm a problem you can't wish away

I beg for change
    That's how I survive
But to you, I'm lower than dirt
    And not fit to be alive

I once had a job
    Paid over a hundred grand a year
But look at me now
    I can't even afford a beer

I'm invisible to you
    You look the other way
But be careful my friend
    This could be you some day

I cry in the night

Jonathan Pasco, Sr.

  Though these tears,
  They're not for me

They are for God's children

  On the street
  Whom you care not to see.

A Discovery at the Fair

At the county fair in an exhibit hall
  I found a little room
It was dark, empty and gloomy with faces on the wall
  It reminded me of a tomb

In the corner sat a man
  Who read poetry to me
Memories of people and places
  And dreams that used to be

He spoke of clouds, of majestic mountains
  And the allure of the sea
Of teddy bears, of children, of Indians
  And a woman who couldn't see

Others wandered in the room out of curiosity
  But none would break the quietude
  Of his sanctuary

We sat spellbound like wide-eyed children
  As the stories would unfold
And for a short time, we were in his world
  Our imaginations were his to hold

To bring a smile to someone's face
  Was his philosophy
But to awaken the passion in a stranger's heart
  Is how his poetry reached out to me.
We left that place when he had finished
  Our hearts a little lighter
I guess he accomplished what he wanted to do
  By making someone's day
    A little brighter

Jonathan Pasco, Sr.

Thoughts of You

Missing you is an understatement

      Like a dying man in the desert
         Misses a cool sip of water

      Like a caged eagle
         Misses soaring above the clouds

      Or two lovers
         Missing the stars and moon in the sky
           On a rainy and dark foggy night

I miss you with every breath I take
      Every move I make
      And every thought that flashes through my mind

If I were to fall dead right now…
      There would be a smile on my lips

Because my last dying thought
      Would be of you.

Jonathan Pasco, Sr.

Carol Hogan

Carol Hogan has been writing poetry since her teens but says she wasn't brave enough to read her poetry out loud till she reached her fifties. With that she will laugh and then proceed to read poetry that reaches into our hearts and finds those spaces left untouched and often unknown. Carol was raised on the beaches of Southern California and traveled from coast to coast until she settled in the Valley of the Sun, Phoenix, Arizona. She laughs as she cries, she roars her protests to life's indignities and brings with her a taste of what she calls, "California Hippydom." Of course this is followed with her own laughter. She has two self-published chapbooks of poems and has traveled to many states to read her work. Additionally, she is active in promoting and supporting new poets and those who are reading poetry for the first time. It is her hope that writers will step forward and bring to the stage more of their own human experience. To make this happen, Carol has hosted several open readings in the Phoenix area, one, "Poetry in the Park – Encanto Series," was the longest running poetry venue in Phoenix. Carol has served on the executive board of the Arizona State Poetry Society for many years as its Treasurer and was Chair of the ASPS 2012 Fall Poetry Contest and Annual Fall Conference held in mid-November 2012.

Keyboard Brainstorm

Rains fall and thunder rolls
Lightning accents a muddy sky
I'm holed up here in my cave and thinking
I'd be walking along the beach,
if I could ...
Watching the rain drill little holes in the wet sand;
I'd be sipping a cup of joe at Java Jungle in Ocean
Beach
Sitting just under the canvas cover,
if I could ...
Watching the deluge fill the kaleidoscope of pots filled
with green
Big drops bouncing high in the lap of a cement lion's
face;
I'd be walking in the tall sequoia woods,
if I could ...
Listening as the rain drops caromed from leaf to
branch
Echoing clicking noises as it fell to the ground;
I'd be standing in the street with arms outstretched
Face lifted to the dark night ... mouth agape as
I caught the blessed cool from the heavens,
if I could ...
Yet alas ... here I am at my keyboard
saying goodnight to friends across the ether.
Here's to ya' and true hopes of wet in your world ...

Carol Hogan

Mother Moon

Resonant celtic chords permeate the room
Sweet smells of incense lace the air
Wine decanted, glasses gleaming
Strawberries, red and succulent

Heavens' indigo velvet beckons from my balcony
Blue so deep it devours my soul
Distant lights, the horizon a string of diamonds
The caress of a rare desert breeze

Shimmering shard of moonlight
Creeps slowly across the floor
Now touching my toes
Then covering my naked feet

It's time -- a time so special,
A time not often shared
When body croons to the caress of moonlight
Naked, stands gilded in heavenly crystal

We stand together in silent communion
This wondrous sphere and I
Full, white and glorious she speaks
Face raised and arms wide I greet her
Still sweet, still whole, still magnificent
Liquid night races to the dawn
Mother moon's only question echoes mine
Where are you?

Carol Hogan

Sitting out the Storm

Storms without
Storms within
Heavens explode
Seas roil
My favorite place is
A warm hearth,
A good book and

A warm cuppa hope.

Lois Requist

Lois Requist, current poet laureate of Benicia, has found the path to her life through writing. Maybe it's cheap therapy, but writing out whatever disturbs her peace of mind brings her...serenity! She was trained in the creative writing program at San Francisco State University in the '80s and has numerous publications, including two books: *Where Lilacs Bloom* and *RVing Solo Across America . . .without a cat, dog, man, or gun*. She finds pleasure in reading, walking, everyday life, travel, her children and grandchildren, and her friends. She enjoys being with kind, thoughtful, smart, and fun people. Her website: www.rvingsolo.com.

Clearing Out   (for Larry)

It was just your stuff
Crammed in every drawer, closet
Under and on top, hanging
In plastic bags from knobs
And other unlikely places

That accumulation
Followed you like a faithful dog

Then you died…
We let that settle awhile

Your stuff
Now the memorabilia of you
Endless pads of paper, your handwriting
On the first line and page
A few scrawled sentences
And you were done

We pause to read the words
We had no time for then
You were a good beginner
A finisher…not so much

Your stuff energized
Picture puzzles never assembled
Tape recordings of the Bible
Pictures of the Grand Canyon
Bars and bars of soap
You never scrubbed with

It's a weighty thing we do
Clearing out your home
Here where you keeled over

Gone, the paramedic said, "like that"
"Didn't feel a thing"

We always saw your limitations
Your capabilities…not so much
Sometimes we were ashamed of you
You didn't know when to stop eating
Or to cease working and helping when you wanted to
When something tickled you, the laughter bubbled up
and over

I see you standing near the doorway
The mystery we never solved
A tentative smile on your face

The past tense that now
Always will follow your name

The Postcard

Your mind travels first and sends back a postcard.
You grab it, glad for a paper adventure. The gravel
road becomes pebbled perfection. You forget the
gray people and grim skies, hunting for the sun
tan oil, a little high from the rum you sip at sunset,
saying to yourself, someday, I too must go there
to see if reality got it right. You are all I thought
you would be, but the luggage was lighter.

On the Water's Edge

Walking along its edge
I see posts, old pilings, parts of piers
Little houses on the water
History gathers here

Not only mine
Drawn here from a dry Idaho
An irrigated desert
Those who earlier lived on this edge
Fished, grew babies, brothels, and bars
Churches, too, schools

The water's edge
Has always pulled humans
Like the moon's tidal tug
For food or fish or possibilities
Of what connects and what separates us
The sun and moon rise here
Sometimes the moon sends its beams
Slithering orange across the water

It is good to walk and live and be part
Of now and the past

To spot a ship on the horizon
Sails billowing my imagination
With what will be after
Along this edge

Brett Hudson

Brett Hudson lives in Benicia and does construction work, as well as writing poetry and playing guitar.

Within

By myself I stand alone
Isolated on these weary feet I roam and emotions are
high and feelings are low
I just don't know which way to go
In searching for a better way I kneel upon the earth
and pray
As I turn to God and ask for help
I find within myself
God's spirit is within me
living God's will shall set me free.
I am no longer alone
I'm walking a path, with God I roam.

Heaven Sent

She has a beauty that can't be explained
Vibrant with energy yet seems so tame.
Her skin so soft, so smooth when I touch her,
It's the way she moves.
Letting me know to love her some more,
She was sent from Heaven of that I'm sure,
For the love she gives, so sweet and pure!
If I were an artist her picture I'd paint,
She has the grace of an angel and
The heart of a saint.

Feelings

Feelings that bring me up
Feelings bring me down
Feelings running through me, at twice the speed of sound
Feelings of love
Feelings of pain
Feelings that broke my heart, will I ever be the same
Feelings I hang on to
Feelings I let go
Feelings I don't understand
Yet feelings help me grow!

Emotions

Emotions to me are like the tide
Sometimes they run low, sometimes they run high
They seem to flow through me and then they subside
Yet they always return
Where do they hide?

Brett Hudson

Joanette Sorkin

Joanette Sorkin is a physician stationed at Travis Air Force Base, where she is Chief of Psychiatry. She lives in Benicia with two cats, four apple, three plum, two cherry, a nectarine, an apricot, a pomegranate and two pear trees (no partridge). Before moving to the land of fruits and nuts, she lived in the land of the midnight sun, where she served at the Alaska Native Medical Center and Southcentral Foundation. In addition to medicine and gardening, her interests include skate skiing, bicycling, and of course, poetry.

Attractive Nuisance

What if the move I've made is wrong
And we both pay the price?
Internal judges sound the gong
If the move I've made is wrong
Although I'll sing a sadder song
I had to roll the dice.
What if the move I've made is wrong
And we both pay the price?

If chemistry is not enough
And someday we are split
We've had some smooth before the rough
If chemistry is not enough
If honeyed words turn grim or gruff
You'll still be hard to quit
If chemistry is not enough
And someday we are split

Although the odds don't favor it
This could work out all right.
At least we get to savor it
Although the odds don't favor it
Experience can flavor it
to taste both rich and light.
Although the odds don't favor it
This could work out all right.

Joanette Sorkin

Homage to His Coy Mistress

Had we but world enough and time,
This chitchat, sir, would be no crime.
We'd eat and talk of many things,
Grand cuisine, the shape of wings;
You could impress me with your wealth,
I'd wait to test your strength and health.
You'd meet my parents, judge my art,
And I could wait until you start
To wonder what a day'd be like
Without an email aimed to strike
Your fancy or to praise your wit;
We'd have the time to dine and sit.
And you should, if you please, ignore
My overtures, walk out the door
And saunter back when timing suits,
When other goals have borne their fruits;
When cell phones needn't interrupt
Nor traffic stall nor work disrupt
Your plan for taking lots of time
Before you must decide your mind.

But at my back I always hear
Time's winged chariot hurrying near.
How long before you need Cialis?
Lose your hair, take on ballast?
Your bike won't ride itself up hills
When beta blockers limit thrills.
When muscles weaken, balance wanes,
When movement's fraught with aches and pains,
Money won't buy back the time
You missed while you were in your prime.
They'll press to guide your teet'ring tread
But few will lead you to their bed.

      Now therefore, while you're at full height,
Solid built and burning bright;

While sinews stretch and pulse can quicken,
Let us seize the chances given,
And like two children playing truant,
Skip our chores until we're fluent
In languages of touch and tremor;
Seeking, finding merged together.
And though we can't bring back what's lost,
Or keep the future free from cost,
We'll lose ourselves, no I or thou,

Transcended by the here, the now.

Joanette Sorkin

The Keys Please

I've found an extra set of keys
With luck, they may unlock my heart
I hold them out as if to tease
Though giving them may not be smart

With luck, they may unlock my heart
If you take mine, I'll have yours please
Though giving them may not be smart
The need's not easy to appease

If you take mine, I'll have yours please
I hope the horse precedes the cart
The need's not easy to appease
Be gentle, I could fall apart

I hope the horse precedes the cart
I hold them out as if to tease
Be gentle, I could fall apart
I've found an extra set of keys

Joanette Sorkin

Deborah B. Silverman

Deborah Silverman was born and raised in Washington, D. C., where the seasons were defined by election politics, school, cherry blossoms on the tidal basin, and sweltering summer nights on the sleeping porch. With backgrounds in philosophy, education, and health science, she eventually settled on psychology. She is now retired from her private practice as a psychologist and as an associate clinical professor at UC San Francisco. Her experiences of the '60s, as well as life abroad and many moves and travel adventures, help to inform her more recent interest in poetry. Now it is the passages of their children and grandchild that help mark the seasons for Deborah and her high school sweetheart, who have been married almost fifty-five years.

Death of an Uncle

"Two small steaks, lean, no sauce."
She ordered brusquely for them both.
As seniors, they knew precisely what they liked.
"And be sure they're well done."

She, even as a young wife, had been elderly,
emulating her old-world mother.
In her '50's housedress and wrap-around apron,
she adhered to a rigorous cleaning schedule
and a weekly dinner routine,
micro-managed compliant children.

He had more spunk when young,
loving sports and music, the company of women,
but was from similar stock as she,
and when it came right down to it,
became his father, married his mother.

They lived their years together
on a tract housing cul-de-sac,
their split-level awash with grey light,
devoid of art, artifacts, or keepsakes.

They vacationed in Hershey, PA,
where one presumes they departed from regimen,
surreptitiously sampling the richness of chocolate.

Otherwise, no risks, no sin, no drama –
at least that anyone knew.

He became ill – not, mind you, gravely ill
but "grey-ly" ill - overcast, leaden, not well.
He stopped wanting to eat anything at all.
Life didn't taste good.

He had done his time, spent his youth,
subsisted as dutiful husband, doting father,
dreary bureaucrat, quiet retiree.
His juices were all dried up. He was, well, done.

Deborah B. Silverman

To Journey

to take the pulse of our atmosphere
synchronize my heart with its energy
subsist within its eternal memory
get a beat on the living being that is home

home to the fish and the mountain goat
to coral and lava, granite and sand
to sturdy pine and gossamer fern
to luminous waters, dark fertile earth

to woven hut and carved temple
to the sinew of continents and islands
the many cultures that are the organs
vibrating in harmony and dis-ease

I wish to release the tired breath
of my own microscopic life
and with eyes, ears and every pore
breathe in the fullness of the world

Don't Teach Me Nothing

suppose that attempting a
little dinner conversation
the coming-of-age daughter
this child teacher
explains that her father's
double negatives
cancel one another out

and suppose that the father
ire rising
rising from his chair
in a fire of indignation
with bellowing gesticulations
flood of furious defiance

berates his daughter
attacks the lesson
becomes instructor
teaches his teacher
the veracity of double negatives

Deborah B. Silverman

Two Postcards from Laos

1. VILLAGE VOICE
our darkly burnished boat
slid along the muddy Mekong
passing village after hidden village
dense silence broken yet again
by attenuated calls of children
grouped on the high shore
colorful specks amid the rough bark
of giant tree trunks
walnut skin blending with a
raw weave of homes behind
babes new as the monsoon's offering
of silt at water's edge
living lives as old as the river
primeval in comforts and spare of dreams
asking only for a wave of our hand
waiting merely to be acknowledged

2. VILLAGE RIDE
I was not walking, I was trudging;
it was not hot, it was sweltering,
this was not a vehicle, it was a pushcart
on which one boy was giving two others a ride.
But I climbed on, and all three of them,
giggling and straining,
thrust the antique wagon into motion.
Young women, tending babies
in the shade under stilted homes,
laughed openly in amusement
as I was hauled, like a pig to market,
down the rough, mile-long dirt path
to the edge of the village,
and adeptly delivered
to my waiting boat on the Mekong,
only my pride left behind.

Deborah B. Silverman

www.ingramcontent.com/pod-product-compliance
Lightning Source LLC
Chambersburg PA
CBHW030602020526
44112CB00048B/1182